Counting Petals

Using Flowers of Hawai'i

by:

NANCY C. WHITMAN

Photographs by:

LUTHER CHONG
HUAN MA
NANCY C. WHITMAN
EDWARD YEE
PATRICIA FOO PATON
GARY K. WONG

Gotham Books

30 N Gould St.
Ste. 20820, Sheridan, WY 82801
https://gothambooksinc.com/

Phone: 1 (307) 464-7800

© 2023 *Nancy C. Whitman.* All rights reserved.

No part of this book may be reproduced, stored in a retrieval system, or transmitted by any means without the written permission of the author.

Published by Gotham Books (November 29, 2023)

ISBN: 979-8-88775-372-0 (P)
ISBN: 979-8-88775-373-7 (E)

Because of the dynamic nature of the Internet, any web addresses or links contained in this book may have changed since publication and may no longer be valid.

The views expressed in this work are solely those of the author and do not necessarily reflect the views of the publisher, and the publisher hereby disclaims any responsibility for them.

DEDICATION

This book is dedicated to children around the world.

I acknowledge the help I received from the staff at Kapi'olani Community College and the Lyon Arboretum of the University of Hawai'i in obtaining photos and for the identification of plants. I thank my neighbors for letting me take pictures of the lovely flowers in their yards.

Special thanks to Freddie Sanchez, Luther Chong, and Jo Diamond for helping me with the technology of photography.

TEACHING TIPS

1. Encourage the child to look for patterns among photos on a particular page.

2. Encourage the child to recognize sets of objects of twos, threes, and possibly fours without counting.

3. Help the child to count in a circular fashion by suggesting a starting petal. A finger may be placed on it to keep track of the first petal counted.

4. Be sure you model matching the numerals: 1,2,3...to the petals.

5. Note that the last numeral named in the matching process is the number of objects in the entire set.

6. Help the child to recognize the multiples of two, that is to recognize:

    four is two times two,
    six is three times two,
    eight is four times two,
    ten is five times two.

7. Encourage the child to recognize that

    two groups of three objects are the same as three groups of two objects,
    two groups of four objects are the same as four groups of two objects,
    two groups of five objects are the same as five groups of two objects.

Counting Petals

Using Flowers of Hawai'i

**WHAT NUMBER IS COMMON
TO ALL THESE FLOWERS? EXPLAIN.**

'APE

BUTTERFLY ANTHURIUM

SPATHIPHYLLUM

ANTHURIUM

1 ONE

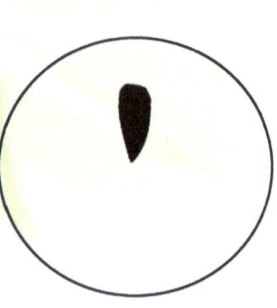

WHAT NUMBER DOES EACH PHOTOGRAPH HAVE IN COMMON?

HELICONIA

CROWN OF THORNS

LEHUA

BLUE AMAZON

2 TWO

**WHAT IS COMMON AMONG
THE THREE PHOTOGRAPHS? EXPLAIN.**

YELLOW GINGER

HELICONIA

CALLA

WHITE GINGER

3 THREE

FOR EACH PHOTOGRAPH
COUNT THE NUMBER OF PETALS.

FOR EACH FLOWER
COUNT THE NUMBER OF PETALS.
ARE 2 AND 2 EQUAL TO 4? EXPLAIN.

HYDRANGEA

CROWN OF THORNS

BLUE AMAZON

IXORA

4 FOUR

EXPLAIN HOW THE FLOWERS ARE ALIKE.

PLUMERIA

ALLAMANDA

VINCA

CUP OF GOLD

MOTH ORCHID

WHITE HIBISCUS

5 FIVE

WHAT DOES EACH OF THE FLOWERS
HAVE IN COMMON?

HOW MANY GROUPS OF TWO
ARE IN EACH FLOWER?

HOW MANY GROUPS OF THREE
ARE IN EACH FLOWER?

ZEPHYR

SPIDER LILY

COLORED LILY

TAHITIAN GARDENIA

DAY LILY

6 SIX

**EXPLAIN HOW THE
TWO FLOWERS ARE ALIKE.**

HELICONIA

COSMOS

TAHITIAN GARDENIA

7 SEVEN

HOW ARE THE PICTURES SIMILAR? EXPLAIN HOW
THE PETALS IN THE CROWN OF THORNS ARE GROUPED.
EXPLAIN HOW THE PETALS IN THE IXORA ARE GROUPED.
DO YOU SEE ANY LINES OF SYMMETRY?
DO YOU SEE ANY ROTATIONAL SYMMETRY?

CROWN OF THORNS

IXORA

HELICONIA

STAR JASMINE

8 EIGHT

**HOW ARE THE THREE FLOWERS ALIKE?
HOW MANY GROUPS OF THREE ARE IN EACH FLOWER?**

WEDELIA

STAR JASMINE

ARABIAN JASMINE

HELICONIA

9 NINE

WHAT IS SIMILAR ABOUT ALL THE PICTURES?
EXPLAIN WHY 2 GROUPS OF 5 IS THE SAME AS 5 GROUPS OF 2?

CROWN OF THORNS

PASSION FRUIT

PUA KENIKENI

ARABIAN JASMINE

10 TEN

SOME POSSIBLE RESPONSES

1. One. They all have one petal.
2. The number 2.
3. They all have three parts or petals.
6. Each flower has 6 petals. Three groups of 2. Two groups of 3.
8. Each photo has 8 petals. The crown of thorns is grouped by 2s. The ixora is grouped by 4s.
9. They all have 9 petals.
10. Each photo has 10 petals.
When two groups of 5 and 5 groups of 2 are counted, they are both ten.

FLOWER GLOSSARY

Allamanda

This flower is called lani-alii, or Heavenly Chief by the Hawaiians. This plant may be a shrub or a vine that covers walls and fences. It is a native of Brazil.

Anthurium

This flower is very popular for use in flower arrangements. The flowers range in size and in color from white to pink to red, and some are green or brown. They appear waxy and seem artificial. Because of their appearance some are called butterfly, Mickey mouse, or obake (ghostly) anthurium.

'Ape

This plant is sometimes referred to as the "elephant ear" plant because of the size and shape of the leaves. The flowers are green-, rose-, and cream-colored and are usually hidden by the leaves. It has an unpleasant smell. This plant is related to the taro plant.

Arabian Jasmine

The flowers of this plant grow on low bushes. It is very similar in appearance to the star jasmine except the stems of the flowers are rounded rather than spike-like as in the star jasmine. The flowers may have 6-10 petals. They are fragrant.

Blue Amazon

This plant is sometimes referred to as "Brazilian snapdragon." The flowers grow profusely in low bushes. This plant may be seen on the road up to Lyon Arboretum in Honolulu.

Calla

This plant is generally found on the island of Hawai'i and is usually white. Flowers may be found on 18–20-inch stems. There are now smaller plants and flowers that are on smaller stems and are pink in color.

Colored Lily

This lily consists of more than one color unlike the day and spider lilies. It does have six petals, a characteristic of lilies.

Crown of Thorns

Thorns grow on the stems of this plant. The flowers appear on the top of the stems in bunches. While traditionally red and small in size, the flowers now are found in a variety of colors and sizes. A magnificent display of these flowers is available at the Kapi'olani Community College in Honolulu. The flowers bloom year-round.

Cosmos

The cosmos shown is commonly referred to as a garden cosmos or Mexican aster. It grows easily in Honolulu.

Cup of Gold

This plant is a large vine with blossoms that bloom in the spring. The blossoms are fragrant, but short-lived. Originally from the West Indies, this plant is a member of the potato family.

Day Lily

This low plant is frequently seen in Hawai'i gardens. As characteristic of lilies, the day lily has six petals. You generally see them growing as clumps of plants making a pretty plant border.

Heliconia

Because they last long the heliconias are frequently found in flower arrangements. There are numerous varieties of this plant. The plants are relatives of the banana plant. When not in bloom they may be mistaken for a clump of banana plants.

Hibiscus

The hibiscus comes in a variety of colors. Since 1988, a yellow hibiscus, *Hibiscus Brackenridgei* became Hawai'i's state flower. The flowers bloom all year and without water remains fresh for a full day after they are picked. The white one may last for two days and has a slight fragrance.

Hydrangea

These plants are commonly given as gifts in pots during the Easter holidays. Its many flowers form a ball of flowers like the ixora plant. The blue color or pink color of the plants depends on the amount of acid in the soil.

Ixora

The individual flowers of this plant form a pompom of color on the plant. The flowers are occasionally used in making leis. The flowers have 4-5 lobes. The plant is a relative of the coffee tree and comes from the East Indies.

Lehua

The lehua pictured is the lehua haole. The blossom resembles the tufted red stamins of the 'ōhi'a lehua. The lehua haole is more frequently seen in yards than the 'ōhi'a lehua. Some trees have white instead of red flowers.

Orchid

The orchid pictured is commonly known as moth, moon, or mariposa orchid. It is widely cultivated as a decorative houseplant. Also referred to as Phalaenopsis.

Orchid-Cymbidium

Seen frequently in flower arrangements. Prefers cool weather to flower. Grown on the island of Hawai'i.

Passion Flower

The Hawaiian name for this flower is liliko'i. The flowers grow on vines that drape trees or sprawl over walls and rocky terrain. The yellow fruit which they produce has a tart taste and is used to make juice, jam, and jellies. This flower comes in a variety of colors.

Plumeria

The plumeria flower comes in a variety of colors. It blooms in spring at the tip of branches and then leaves come out. The plant continues to bloom until the wintertime. The milky sap of this plant is poisonous. This plant can be seen in many gardens in Hawai'i. The flower is very popular for making Hawaiian flower leis.

Puu Kenikeni

This plant is a native of the South Pacific. It grows into a spreading tree about 15 feet tall. The flowers are popular in leis. It is fragrant. The Hawaiian name means "ten cents flower," which is the amount each flower used to cost.

Spathiphyllum

Frequently seen as ground cover in Hawai'i gardens. It is about 18 inches tall. Shorter plants may be seen as houseplants. The houseplants can grow in water. The flowers resemble the anthurium and calla flowers.

Spider Lily

This plant blooms year-round. The flower is white. It has six thin petals and six stamens extending from its center thus making it a member of the lily family.

Star Jasmine

The flowers of this small bush are seen in gardens in Hawai'i. The flower is pin-wheeled shaped and looks like a star. It may have from four to ten petals and has a mild fragrance.

Tahitian Gardenia

This gardenia looks like a pinwheel. The number of petals it has varies from five to

nine. It is very fragrant. The shrub plants are used frequently as hedges in Hawai'i.

Turk's Cap

The bright red pendent, hibiscus-like flower never fully opens with its petals overlapping to form a loose tube. They are used to make leis in Hawai'i.

Vinca

Sometimes this flower is called periwinke. It is a perennial plant that is often used as ground cover in Hawai'i. The flowers bloom nearly year-round. They come in pink, white, and lavender. The flowers have five petals and are 1-2 inches in diameter.

Wedelia

This plant is commonly used as a ground cover in landscaped properties such as banks and schools. Its flowers usually have more than 12 petals.

White Ginger

This flower is very fragrant. It is used in making special leis. They grow along the roadside and in people's yards. It is considered by some as the most romantic of all the gingers because of its fragrance and delicacy.

Yellow Ginger

This flower is very much like the white ginger in appearance except the flower is yellow. Its fragrance is not as delicate as the white ginger and is not found as frequently as the white one in leis.

Zephyr

This is a small, bulbous border plant with grass-like leaves about a foot long. The flowers are similar to the crocus. In Hawai'i the flowers bloom at any time.

COUNTING IN OTHER LANGUAGES

ENGLISH	SPANISH	MANDARIN	HAWAIIAN	JAPANESE	CHINESE NUMERALS
One	Uno	Yi	'Ekahi	Ichi	一
Two	Dos	Er	'Elua	Ni	二
Three	Tres	San	'Ekolu	San	三
Four	Cuatro	Si	'Eha	Yon	四
Five	Cinco	Wu	'Elima	Go	五
Six	Seis	Liu	'Ekono	Roku	六
Seven	Siete	Qi	'Ehiku	Nana	七
Eight	Ocho	Ba	'Ewalu	Hachi	八
Nine	Nueve	Jiu	'Eiwa	Ku	九
Ten	Diez	Shi	'Umi	Ju	十

AUTHOR'S PAGE

Nancy is wearing a Turk's Cap lei.

Nancy is holding Obake Anthirium from her garden.

Nancy is enjoying bouquet with many Cymbidium orchids.

REFERENCES

Anita, Vera. Illustrated by Ruth Moen Cabanting. All Around the Islands. 'Ewa Beach, Hawai'i: BeachHouse Publishing, 2005.

> A counting book in rhyme that introduces some of Hawai'i's most beloved animals—from the humpback whale to the gecko to the soaring 'iwa—along with each island in the Hawaiian Island chain.

Bess Press. Photography by Mike and Kim Crinella, Caryl Nishioka, Wayne Thomas, and Carol and Tim Starr. Flowers of Hawai'i. Honolulu: Bess Press, 2004.

> A handy folding pamphlet of photographs of flowers of Hawai'i.

Green, Yuko. Ten Little Geckos. Waipahu, Hawai'i: Island Heritage Publishing, 2018.

> Counting is done in reverse starting with number ten.

Hruby, Emile. Illustrated by Patrick Hruby. Counting in the Garden. Ammo Books, 2010.

> Counting from one to twelve is learned by counting objects in a garden such as turnips and thistles.

Forsythe Demming. Illustrated by Mirto Golino. Ten Little Menehunes: A Hawaiian Counting Book. Honolulu: Menehunes.com Publishing, 2000.

> Has pronunciation guide. Has reverse counting.

Hodge, Peggy Hickok. Photography by Peggy Hickok Hodge and Lee R. Hickok. Gardening in Hawai'i: Handbook for the Home Gardener. Honolulu: Mutual Publishing, 1996.

> Interesting write-up of day lilies.

Hargreaves, Dorothy, and Bob. Tropical Blossoms of the Pacific. Lahaina, HI: Ross-Hargreaves, 1970.

>Over 100 full color pictures with descriptions.

Hawaiian Services, Inc. Images of Hawaii's Flowers: A Pictorial Guide to the Aloha's State's Flowering Plants. Honolulu: Hawaiian Services, Inc.,1996.

>Has technical names of flowers. Gives brief descriptions of flowers: ginger, hibiscus, gardenia (Tiara), heliconia, etc.

Imamura, Andrew. 123 Cut Loose in Hawai'i. Kane'ohe, Hawai'i: BeachHouse Publishing, 2021.

>The art of Japanese paper cutting is used to illustrate the sea and land animals of Hawai'i. These animals are named and counted in both English and Hawaiian.

Kaopuiki, Stacey. Bring Me What I Ask. Wailuku, Maui, HawaI'i: Hawaiian Island Concepts, 1991.

>A simple, delightful tale that teaches children numbers in English, Hawaiian, and sign language.

Kawai'ae'a, Keiki Chang. Let's Learn to Count in Hawaiian. Honolulu: Island Heritage Publishing, 1988.

Kepler, Angeler K. . Photography by Jacob R. Mau. Exotic Tropicals of Hawaii. Honolulu: Mutual Publishing, 1989.

>Lot of heliconias, gingers and anthuriums.

Kepler, Angela Kay. Hawai'i's Floral Splendor. Honolulu: Mutual Publishing, 1997.

>Written by a field naturalist. It brings alive the kaleidoscopic floral bounty that beautifies the island's roadsides, parks, resorts, public gardens, beaches, and interior forests.

Kuck, Lorraine E. and Tongg, Richard C. Hawaiian Flowers and Flowering Trees. Tokyo: Tuttle, 1958.

> Has good pictures-probably painted. Good description of the flowers and plants.

McMillan, Bruce. Counting Wildflowers. New York: Lothrop, Lee & Shepard Books, 1986.

> A counting book with photographs of wildflowers illustrating the numbers one to twenty.

Miyano, Leland. Photos by Douglas Peebles. A Pocket Guide to Hawai'i's Flowers. Honolulu: Mutual Publishing, 1997.

Moir, Gertrude M.F. Hawaii's Flowers. GERTRUDE MOIR, 1979.

> Beautiful paintings. Gives short descriptions of the plants.

Outdoor Circle. Trees and Flowers of the Hawaiian Islands. Honolulu: Honolulu Star Bulletin, LTD.

> A beautiful collection of images of trees and flowers of Hawaii.

Partners in Development Foundation. Illustrated by Garrett Omoto. 'Umi Keiki Li'ili'I. Honolulu: Partners in Development Foundation, 2006.

> A counting book to aid children to learn to count in Hawaiian and English. A useful aid to caregivers and teachers.

Parker, Kim. Counting in the Garden. New York: Scholastic, 2005.

Peebles Douglas, photographer and Miyana, Phyllis. Hawai'i a Floral Paradise. Honolulu: Mutual Publishing, 1995.

Seiden Allan. Flowers of Hawaii. Honolulu: Island Heitage, 1985.

> Includes photos and descriptions of hibiscus, anthurium, spider lily, passion flower, allamanda, white ginger, heliconia, stephanosis, ixora.

Wichman, Juliet Rice. Illustrated by Sara Hertford. Moki Learns to Fish. Lihue, Hawai'i: Kauai Museum Association, 1981.

Moki learns to fish with his father and grandfather and also learns to count from one to ten in English and Hawaiian.

www.ingramcontent.com/pod-product-compliance
Lightning Source LLC
LaVergne TN
LVHW070535070526
838199LV00075B/6784